Ancient Greece

Kevin Jane and Priscilla Wood

Published by Collins

An imprint of HarperCollins*Publishers*

The News Building

1 London Bridge Street

London

SE1 9GF

Browse the complete Collins catalogue at
www.collins.co.uk

First published in 2006 by Folens Limited, as part of the *Folens Primary History* series.
Previously published as *A Time to Remember: Ancient Greece*.

10 9 8

ISBN: 978-0-00-746398-5

Acknowledgements

The authors and publisher wish to thank the following for permission to use
copyright material:

Ashmolean Museum, pp18, 19, 20, 21, 29, 31, 35, 51, 53

Bridgeman Art Library, p45 (right)

The Trustees of the British Museum, pp7, 9, 17, 18, 19, 29, 34 (bottom), 35, 43 (top), 44, 52,
53, 54, 55

Corbis, pp4 (top left), 62

Mary Evans Picture Library, pp28, 58 (right), 59 (right), 61 (bottom)

Chris Fairclough, p9

Grosvenor Museum, p6 (top)

Michael Holford, pp6, 9, 16, 17, 18, 19, 21, 28, 29, 31, 40, 41, 46, 47, 49, 50, 52, 53 (bottom)

Photolibrary, pp36, 63

Thomson Holidays, pp4 (bottom left), 5, 7 (centre), 8, 14, 15, 34 (top), 35 (bottom),
42 (top), 43 (middle), 51 (middle)

Paul Walters, pp5, 14, 42

Every effort has been made to trace copyright holders and to obtain their permission for
the use of copyright material. The author and publisher will gladly receive any information
enabling them to rectify any error or omission in subsequent editions.

Editors: Saskia Gwinn and Joanne Mitchell

Layout artist: Suzanne Ward

Illustrations: Images in Design, Trevor Parkin, Tony Randell of Tony Randell Illustration

Cover design: Blayney Partnership

Cover image: Sandro Bannini/CORBIS

Contents

Source A

Greece is a small country (smaller than the United Kingdom), and you can see from the map that part of it is made up of little islands. Many people who live in the UK go to these islands for their holidays.

Aegina is one of the most popular Greek islands for holidays. To get to Aegina you can fly to Athens Airport, go by bus to the port at Piraeus and then take a ferry to the island.

A popular island

Look carefully at the information in this chapter. It has all been taken from holiday brochures.

1. Find the island of Aegina on the map of Greece (**Source C**).
2. Why do you think Aegina is so popular? Make a list of the reasons.
3. Would you like to go there?

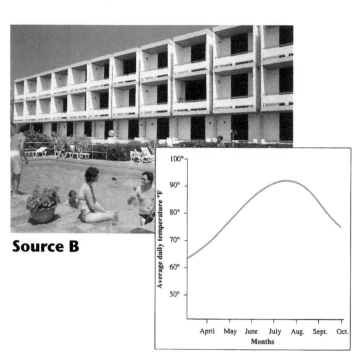

Source B

Source C

This graph shows the temperature in Aegina during the holiday season.

A travel brochure describes how easy it is to reach other parts of Greece from islands such as Aegina.

Frequent ferries make it easy to spend a hot day exploring Athens and to return in the cool of the evening to an island ... You can (also) take the ordinary inter-island boats and hop to Poros, Hydra and Spetsai.

Holiday plans

Imagine you are going to Aegina for your holiday.

1. What time of year would you like to go?
2. Use the information in this chapter to plan how you will spend your time there. Think about where you will stay, what you will see, how you will relax and where you will eat.

The road map of Aghia Marina (**Source D**) shows where the main buildings and tavernas are. Tavernas are small restaurants that serve Greek food, usually very cheaply.

The Apollo is one of the hotels in Aghia Marina. As well as offering food and accommodation, it provides table tennis, mini-golf, tennis, a shop, a restaurant and a rooftop pool with sunbeds. The price chart tells you how much it costs to stay at the hotel for one week. The price also covers the flight to Greece.

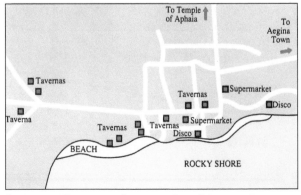

Source D   *Road map of Aghia Marina.*

Date	Adult £	Child £
6–30 April	199	129
1–19 May	210	150
20 May–11 June	299	179
12 June–9 July	329	199
10 July–4 Aug	379	199
5–24 Aug	399	209
25 Aug–10 Sept	329	179
11 Sept–1 Oct	210	130
2–31 Oct	210	150

Source E
Price chart for the Hotel Apollo.

Half the picture

Holiday brochures do not tell us everything about a country. They advertise things for tourists to do.

Do some research to find out how Greeks live in the towns and countryside.

Source F
The Temple of Aphaia.

Source F above shows the Temple of Aphaia. It is a clue as to what you are going to explore in this book. You are going to be historians and try to find out what life was like in Ancient Greece. First, you must journey back in time nearly 3000 years ....

The time line shows some of the major historical events which took place in Ancient Greece. In this book you will be finding out about daily life during the Classical Age.

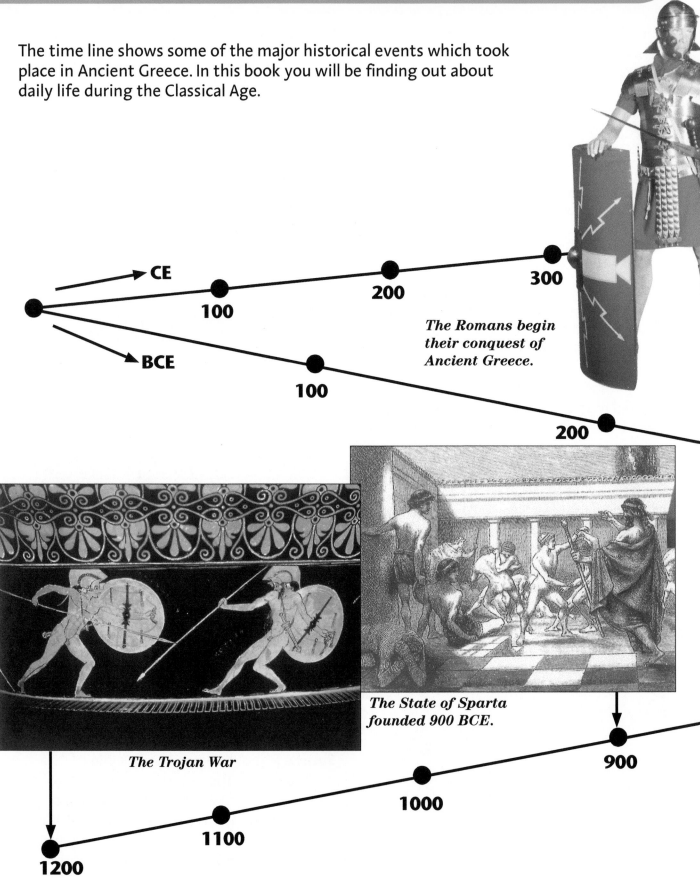

CE

100

200

300

The Romans begin their conquest of Ancient Greece.

BCE

100

200

The Trojan War

The State of Sparta founded 900 BCE.

1200

1100

1000

900

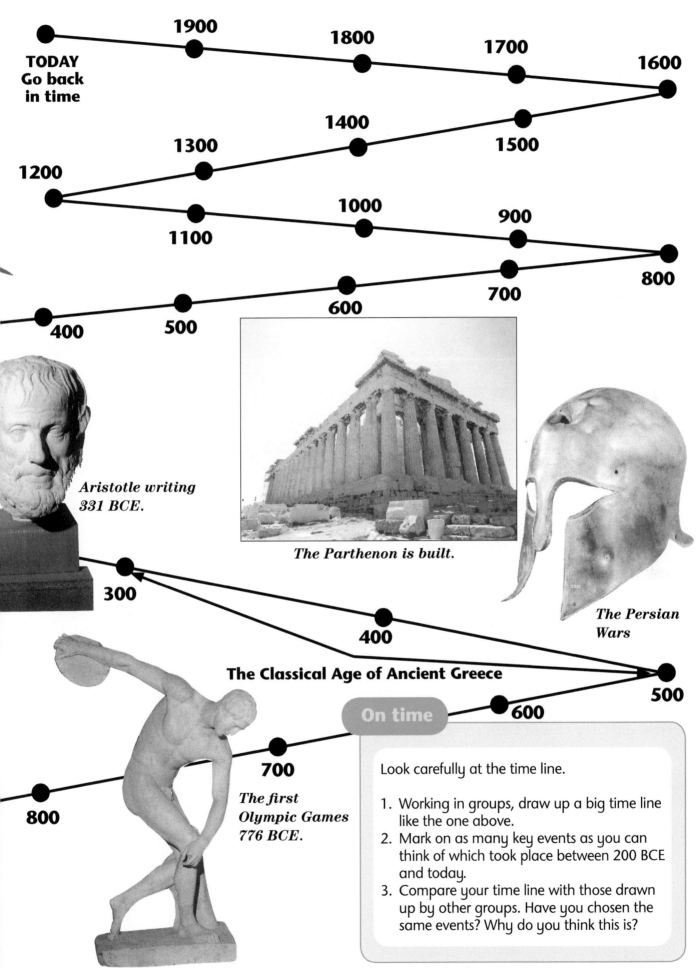

1900
1800
1700
1600

TODAY
Go back
in time

1400
1300
1500

1200

1000
900

1100

800
700

600

400
500

*Aristotle writing
331 BCE.*

The Parthenon is built.

*The Persian
Wars*

300

400

The Classical Age of Ancient Greece

On time

500

600

*The first
Olympic Games
776 BCE.*

700

800

Look carefully at the time line.

1. Working in groups, draw up a big time line
   like the one above.
2. Mark on as many key events as you can
   think of which took place between 200 BCE
   and today.
3. Compare your time line with those drawn
   up by other groups. Have you chosen the
   same events? Why do you think this is?

Source A

To find out how the Ancient Greeks lived, we need to start by asking questions:
- When did they live?
- What did they look like?
- What work did they do?
- How did they amuse themselves?

Asking questions

In groups, discuss what you would like to know about the Ancient Greeks.

Write down a list of all the questions you want to ask.

Living in Ancient Greece

Look at the picture above (**Source A**).

Write down what this picture tells you about how the Ancient Greeks lived. It would be helpful to focus on their leisure time.

Source B

Source C

Source D

To answer questions about the Ancient Greeks you will need to look at evidence. Evidence is anything that has survived from the past that helps us to understand what life was like. The Ancient Greeks left behind many different kinds of evidence such as buildings, jewellery, pottery, writing, bones and pictures.

The picture below shows the British Museum in London. Inside there are a huge number of Ancient Greek artefacts. You may not be able to visit the museum yourself, but in this book you will find many photographs of the objects in the museum.

Sir Arthur Evans and Heinrich Schliemann were two famous archaeologists. They discovered many Ancient Greek buildings and artefacts in the nineteenth century.

Source F

Heinrich Schliemann and Sir Arthur Evans.

Source E *The British Museum in London*

Looking at evidence

Look carefully at the evidence in this chapter.

1. Make a list of the ways we can find out about the people who lived in Ancient Greece.
2. What do the sources provided tell us about the Ancient Greeks?

4 Artefacts

An artefact is something made by people. We can find out about people who lived in the past by looking at the things they made.

Most Ancient Greek artefacts have either decayed, been lost or been destroyed. However, some artefacts have survived and been found by archaeologists. These artefacts are very valuable so they are kept in museums.

As these artefacts are so valuable we cannot hold and look at them. Instead we have to use photographs. On page 11 there are some photographs of artefacts (**Sources A**, **B**, **C** and **D**). In order to learn as much as possible about each artefact, use the sources to consider the questions in the boxes below.

Finding out

Some questions can be answered just by looking at an artefact. Others can be answered by what you already know, by talking to other people, or by looking at books.

1. In pairs, do some research to find answers to the questions in the boxes below.
2. Present your findings. Use words such as 'I think ...' and 'It might ...' unless you are quite certain about your findings. Don't forget to give reasons for your ideas.
3. Compare what you have found out about one artefact with what another person or pair has found out. Have you got the same findings, or are there differences?

Looks

- What does it look like?
- How might it feel, smell or sound?
- What shape and size is it?
- What is it made of?
- Is it complete or is part of it missing?
- Has it been altered or repaired?
- Is it worn?

How it was made

- Was it made by hand or by machine?
- Was it made in a mould or in pieces?
- How many people helped to make it?
- Has it been glued or glazed (given a glassy finish)?
- Has it got a handle, rivets or wires?

Design

- Did the object do what it was supposed to?
- Could it have been better made?
- Is it attractive?
- How is it decorated?

Purpose

- Why was it made?
- Has it been used for anything else?

Value

- Was it worth a lot of money?
- Did it have sentimental value?
- Did it have religious value?

Source A

Source C

Source B

Source D

Source A

The picture above is not only evidence of how women in Ancient Greece spent their leisure time. It also gives us other information about how the Ancient Greeks lived.

Looking closely

As a historian, you must try to find out as much as possible from each historical source.

1. Look carefully at **Source A**. It is a bowl painting and shows some women carrying out day to day activities.
2. Describe what is happening.
3. Write down any questions you have about what is happening.

Everyday life

1. Look carefully at **Source A** again. Discuss what it tells us about:
   ● women's leisure activities
   ● Greek chores
   ● furniture
   ● women's clothes
   ● hairstyles and headdresses.
2. Write about or draw what the picture tells us.

A historian can never be absolutely sure about something just by looking at one piece of evidence. To be certain, we must look for other evidence.

1. Look for evidence to support the ideas you have already recorded. Use your textbook and other books in your classroom and library.
2. Record your findings in a chart like the one below.

Topic	Idea	Evidence to support the idea
Women's clothes	Wore plain brown chitons	**Source A**

Note: You should also make a record if you don't find any supporting evidence. This does not mean that your idea was wrong.

3. Now use a similar way of working to try and answer your questions about the bowl painting on page 12 (**Source A**).

Domestic scene

Source B is part of a vase painting. Use it in the same way as the previous picture to find out about Greek life.

1. Describe what is happening.
2. Write down any questions you have about what is happening.
3. Draw up a list of things the picture tells us.
4. Look for evidence to support your ideas.

Source B

Ancient Greece was not one country with one ruler. It was made up of many small city states. Each city state (called a *polis* in Greek) had an area of high ground on which a temple was built to honour the city's chosen deity (god or goddess). Below the temple were the people's homes and an open area, called the *agora*, which was used for markets and meetings. A wall enclosed the temple, the surrounding buildings and the agora. The countryside outside the walls was used for farming.

Source B

Life was different in each city state. Each state had its own laws and government and there was often fighting between the states.

The two most powerful city states were Athens and Sparta. In Sparta, two royal kings ruled together with the help of a Council of Elders. The kings' main responsibility was to lead the army. A strong army was very important to the Spartans because they had been defeated in several wars and were determined to keep themselves well defended. This system of royal kings and a council is called an *oligarchy*, meaning 'rule by a small group'.

Source A

Setting the scene

Look carefully at **Sources A, B** and **C**. These are photographs of modern Greek landscape.

1. Prepare a page for a tourist brochure explaining the main features of the modern Greek landscape.
2. Which features of Ancient Greece would have been similar?
3. Which features would have been different?

14

Sparta became the strongest city state because of its powerful army. Physical fitness, bravery and fighting skills were very important to the Spartans. Boys were taken from their families at the age of seven and trained to fight. Girls also had to keep fit, so that they would produce strong babies. If a newborn baby was weak it was left to die.

Life in Sparta was harsh and uncomfortable. There is little evidence of any art, music, drama or great architecture in Sparta.

Source C

A Spartan life

Look up the word 'spartan' in a dictionary.

1. What does it mean?
2. How do you think it came to have this meaning?

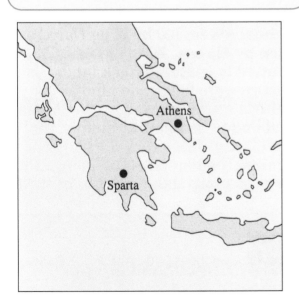

At one time, about 250 000 people lived in the city of Athens and in the surrounding countryside. The people of Athens were not ruled by kings or queens. Instead the citizens ruled themselves. This system is called a *democracy*, meaning 'rule of the people'.

In Athens, every citizen could vote in the assembly place called the *Pnyx*. Here the laws were discussed and voted on. A council made up of 500 men was selected by lot each year, and it was responsible for the day-to-day running of the state. Women, foreign visitors and slaves could not vote. They were not citizens, so they were not allowed to take part in council meetings.

Comparing lifestyles

Read all the information in this chapter about Sparta and Athens.

1. Draw up a table like the one below.
2. Write in the table what you think were some of the good points and bad points of each system.
3. Which city state would you have liked to live in?

	Good points	Bad points
Athens		
Sparta		

The army of each city state was made up of trained citizens. In Athens, all 18 year old male citizens were given two years of military training. In spring, each citizen went to the agora to see if he had been chosen to fight that year. Summer was the season for wars between the city states. The wars were fought to gain land, corn, goats and slaves.

Some soldiers fought on horseback. They were not very efficient because they had no saddle or stirrups. The best soldiers were the foot soldiers called *hoplites*. They were called this because each soldier carried a shield called a *hoplon*. They marched close together with their shields in front, to protect themselves.

Source A

The Greek city states also fought wars against other countries. For nearly 40 years, Athens and other city states were at war with Persia. The Persians were led by King Darius, and then by his son, King Xerxes. They wanted to capture Greek lands. Many battles were fought on land and at sea. Athens was destroyed by the Persians, and had to be rebuilt. Finally, the Greek city states won the long war against the Persians and many Greek writers wrote about what happened.

Armour and weapons

Look carefully at all the sources in this chapter. They show the weapons and armour of wealthy soldiers.

1. Describe the clothes worn by the Ancient Greeks to protect themselves in battle.
2. What sort of weapons did they use?
3. How do you think the weapons and armour of the poor soldiers differed from those of the rich?

The Greeks often fought at sea, as well as on land. *Triremes* (war galleys) were fast, efficient and easy to handle. They carried crews of up to 200 men.

The playwright, Aeschylus, described the result of a sea-battle:

Many of the Persian ships capsized and we could hardly see the surface of the water for wreckage and drowned sailors. Soon every nearby beach was black with Persian corpses.

Source C

Source B

Fighting at sea

Look at the vase painting above in **Source B**.

1. Decide which is the trireme and which is the merchant ship. (Remember, the merchant ship had to be big enough to carry cargo.)
2. How were the triremes powered?
3. Look at the bow (front) of the trireme for clues as to how the ship attacked other boats.
4. Read the extract from the play by Aeschylus. What do you think the Greeks tried to do to other ships and why?

Investigations

Use your school library or resource centre to find out about the following:

– the Battle of Salamis (a naval battle between the Greeks and Persians)
– the Battle of Marathon (a land battle between the Athenians and the Persians)
– The Peloponnesian War (between Athens and Sparta)
– Alexander the Great.

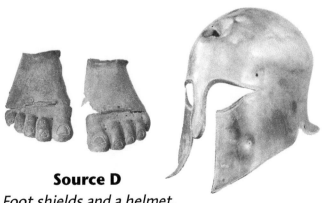

Source D
Foot shields and a helmet.

(8) Houses

Archaeologists have found the remains of many large public buildings, but very few remains of people's homes. With so little evidence it is difficult to know exactly what a typical Ancient Greek house looked like. The houses were built of sun-dried mud bricks which were laid directly on the earth, without any foundations. Even the houses of rich and important people were very simple.

However, there is a lot of evidence to show us what life was like inside Greek homes. Statues and paintings give us clues as to how people cooked, ate, entertained themselves, washed, cleaned their houses and cared for their children.

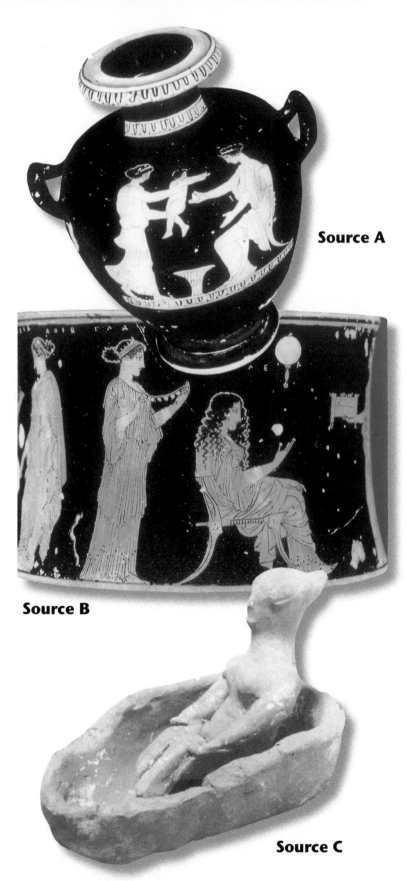

Source A

Source B

Source C

The buildings

Most Greek houses were built to house large families. Grandparents, children, aunts, uncles, cousins and slaves all lived together in one building.

1. Why do you think there are so few remains of these houses?
2. Draw a sketch to show how you think these houses may have looked on the outside.

Household activities

Look carefully at all the sources in this chapter.

1. What activities are taking place?
2. In which rooms do you think these activities took place?
3. Make a list of the rooms that each house may have had.
4. Now look at the picture on page 23 showing the inside of a house. Decide where each room on your list may have been. Explain your decisions.

Source D

Source E

Work in the Home

If we use Ancient Greek art as evidence, we can find out about the type of work carried out in the home.

Household tasks

Draw up a chart like the one below.

1. Discuss all the jobs that you think had to be done in a Greek home.
2. List them in the first column of the chart. After you have completed this column, look at the questions, which follow in the box below.

Jobs done in the home	Evidence found	Who did the work?
Cooking		

Source B

Source A

Finding the evidence

Now, look carefully at **Sources A**, **B**, **C**, **D**, **E** and **F** in this chapter.

1. Can you find any evidence to suggest that the jobs on your list were done in the home?
2. Record any evidence in the second column of your chart.

Jobs done in the home	Evidence found	Who did the work?
Cooking	Statue	

In Ancient Greece there were free people and slaves. Slaves were owned by rich people and worked as servants in their homes and on their farms. Some slaves were bought from traders, others were captured in war. They often lived and worked closely with the family. Many of the household jobs would have been done by slaves.

Source D

Source C

Summarise the evidence

Use your chart and the information in this chapter.

1. Prepare a written summary about the work done in an Ancient Greek home. Remember to say who did the work and what evidence you found. In your summary you can include jobs that were not on your list, if you have evidence for them.
2. Now present your findings in a different way.

Who did the work?

Look closely at the sources again. Can you tell who is doing the work?

1. Is it a man or a woman?
2. Do you think it is a free person or a slave?
3. Record your decisions in the third column of your chart.

Jobs done in the home	Evidence found	Who did the work?
Cooking	Statue	A woman, maybe a slave

Source E

We are very lucky that the Ancient Greeks painted so many pictures on their vases. These paintings give us a lot of evidence about their everyday lives.

1. Look carefully at the painting in **Source F**. You can draw the chair as it is in the painting (see **Figure A**), or you can draw it as it would look if no one was sitting on it (see **Figure B**).
2. Practise sketching your own pictures from the vase painting.

Figure A

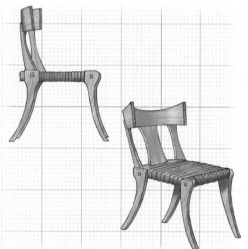

Source F

Figure B

We can use evidence from different sources to build up a detailed picture of what life was like.

1. Use the outline on the next page (**Source G**) as a guide to draw a picture of what life was like inside an Ancient Greek house. Look at pictures on vases in your textbook and other books in your library to give you ideas.
   Do not copy the paintings exactly. Use parts of different paintings to create your own scenes. Plan your drawing before you start. Think about:
   ● which rooms might be in the house
   ● where the women, children, men and slaves might be
   ● what the people might be doing.
2. Now use this way of working to illustrate your favourite Ancient Greek poem or story, or a scene from a Greek play.

Source G

(10) Slaves

All but the very poorest of the Ancient Greeks kept slaves to work in their homes. Slaves also worked on the farms, in the mines and in small businesses, such as shoe-making and pottery.

Men, women and children could be slaves. Some people became slaves when they were captured in war. Others became slaves when they were abandoned at birth or if their parents were slaves.

The slaves who worked in the mines had the hardest lives. They worked long hours in unhealthy conditions. Some slaves who had skilled jobs were paid for their work. The slaves who worked in people's houses were sometimes well treated and allowed to live closely with the family.

Some slaves were Greeks from other city states, but most slaves came from other countries.

Questions to consider

Discuss the following questions in groups of four.

1. What sort of jobs do you think the slaves might have had to do?
2. Would free men and their families have had so much leisure time if they did not have slaves?
3. Do you think that a slave who had been captured might have felt differently to a slave who had been born into slavery?
4. What special problems might a Greek slave have had working for a Greek owner?
5. What special problems might a foreign slave have had working for a Greek owner?

The slavery debate

1. Read the sources on the next page (**Sources A** and **B**). They show that not all Greeks agreed with slavery.

2. Split into two pairs. You are going to be Ancient Greeks discussing the rights and wrongs of slavery. Choose some Greek names for yourselves.

3. Pair A: you are in favour of slavery. Use the information on this page and **Sources A** to give reasons for your belief. Give some advice on how to treat slaves.

4. Pair B: you are against slavery. Use the information on this page and **Sources B** to give reasons for your belief. You will have to try and see slavery from the slaves' point of view.

5. When each pair has prepared its argument, it should present its views to the other pair, trying to convince each other that its point of view is the right one.

Sources A

'A man should own the best and most docile slaves he can get.'
(Plato, *The Laws*)

'We should certainly punish slaves if they deserve it.'
(Plato, *The Laws*)

'Virtually everything you say to a slave should be an order, and you should never become familiar with them.'
(Plato, *The Laws*)

'Yes, it's only the name of slave that carries disgrace with it; in every other point a loyal slave is as good as a free man.'
(Slave in *Ion* by Euripides)

'The use ... of slaves hardly differs at all from that of domestic animals; from both we derive that which is essential for our bodily needs.'

'It is clear ... that by nature some are free, others slaves, and that for these it is both right and expedient that they should serve as slaves.'
(Aristotle)

Sources B

'Zeus but it's hard being a slave when your master's out of his mind. You can give the best advice in the world, but if your owner disagrees, you have to take the consequences of his actions! Fate's made your body not your own – it belongs to the man who buys you.'
(Carion, a slave in *Wealth* by Aristophanes)

'Some people don't trust slaves as a class in anything: they treat them like animals, and whip and goad them so that they make the souls of their slaves three times – no, a thousand times – more slavish than they were. Others follow precisely the opposite policy.'
(Plato, *The Laws*)

'Slavery,
That thing of evil, by its nature evil,
Forcing the submission from man to what
No man should yield to.'
(Euripides)

'Servants, when their masters are no longer there to order them about, have little will to do their duties as they should. All-seeing Zeus takes away half the good out of a man on the day he becomes a slave.'
(A slave in Homer's Odyssey XVII)

'If they're as unhappy as they look
I'm sorry for them ... .
I am full of pity at this sad sight,
These poor unhappy exiles, homeless, fatherless,
Waifs in a strange land – daughters of free-born families,
For all we know, and now condemned to slavery.'
(Deianeira in *Women of Trachis* by Sophocles)

11 The Role of Women

Weighing up the evidence

Read the three statements below.

- Women were treated like slaves.
- Women were more important than slaves, but less important than men.
- Women were equal with men.

1. From what you already know about women in Ancient Greece, which description do you think is the most accurate?

2. Work with someone who has chosen the same statement. Draw up a chart like the one below.

Idea:	
Supports our idea	**Challenges our idea**

3. Read all the pieces of evidence on page 27. They tell us what life was like for women.

4. Cut out the boxes on page 27.

5. Decide which pieces of evidence support (agree with) your idea and which challenge (disagree with) your idea.

6. Put each piece of evidence into the correct column on your chart. (See below for an example.)

Idea: Women were equal with men	
Supports our idea	**Challenges our idea**
Women could become priestesses	Women were not citizens

Note: There may be some pieces of evidence that you cannot decide about. Put these at the end.

7. When you have finished, look at your completed chart. Are there lots of pieces of evidence that support your idea? Are there not many or not any pieces of evidence that challenge your idea? If so, then you can conclude that your idea was correct.

If there are not many pieces of evidence to support your idea, and more pieces of evidence that challenge it, then you may have to change your idea.

8. At the bottom of your work, write a sentence or two to explain what you have found out.

9. Talk to some of your friends who started with a different idea. What have they found out?

You can use this way of working to try out other ideas you may have about the Ancient Greeks.

'... the wife is never present at dinner, unless it is a family party, and spends all her time in a remote part of the house called the women's quarter ...'
Cornelius Nepos, *Lives of Distinguished Generals*

In Athens, women, like slaves, were not citizens and so they could not vote on how the city state should be run.

A woman's husband was chosen for her by her father. A man chose his own wife.

Women held their own games every four years at Olympia. These were called the Heraia, in honour of the goddess Hera.

A wife spent most of her time in the house. It was her job to run the household, which was often quite large.

In Aristophanes' play, The Assembly Women, the women of Athens take over the government of the city in order to save it. The play is a comedy.

Almost all of the dramatists, poets and philosophers that we know about were men.

Men decided whether their newborn babies were strong enough to be allowed to live, or whether they should be left to die.

Women in Greek legends are mostly faithful, loving, thoughtless and not very clever.

In *The Laws*, Plato says that girls should receive the same education as boys, including learning how to fight and use weapons. '... as between male and female, the former is by nature superior and ruler, the latter inferior and subject.'
Aristotle

Women were not allowed to take part in or to watch the Olympic Games.

The gods and goddesses were as powerful as each other. Athena, for example, was very wise, and she could not be beaten in a fight.

Women could become priestesses. This was a very important position to hold.

It was very rare for girls to go to school to be taught to read and write. Most boys were taught reading, writing and some arithmetic.

In all but the poorest households, the wife was responsible for the slaves who did the hardest and most unpleasant jobs in the house.

Men in Greek legends are mostly heroic, courageous, strong and ambitious.

Some of the great characters of Greek tragedies are women. Antigone, for example, in Sophocles' play is very noble and brave. She does what she believes is right even though she knows she will die because of it.

A modern picture showing what a Spartan school might have been like.

In Ancient Greece, the father of a newborn baby had to decide whether to let the baby live or die. If a baby looked weak or unhealthy it was left to die. This may seem cruel to us, but remember that there were no hospitals and few medicines in Ancient Greece.

If the father decided that the baby was healthy enough to survive, a special naming ceremony was held. This ceremony was called the *amphidromia*, and it welcomed the child into the family.

Babies and toddlers

Look at the artefact and picture opposite (**Sources A** and **B**).

1. What do you think each object was used for?
2. Do we use anything similar today?

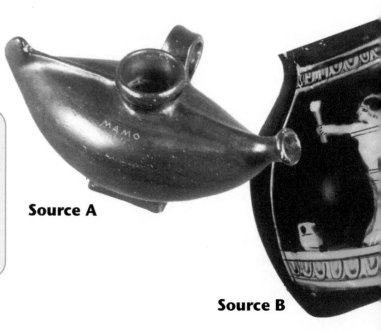

Source A

Source B

Celebrating a child

There are many types of celebration to welcome a new baby into its family or community.

How many different celebrations can you think of?

Most Greek girls were taught at home, usually by their mothers. Girls were often married at the age of 15. Their husbands were chosen for them by their fathers.

Education for girls

Think about the role of women in the home (see chapter 11).

1. What skills did girls need to learn to prepare them for their adult lives?
2. How does a girl's education today differ from that in Ancient Greece?
3. Are there any similarities?
4. Look carefully at **Sources C**, **D** and **E**. Can you identify these Ancient Greek toys? Do children today have similar toys?

In Ancient Greece, children were educated to prepare for their adult roles. This meant that boys were educated differently from girls. It also meant that the education varied from state to state.

In Athens, boys were taught basic arithmetic and how to read and write. Many were taught by private tutors, who may have been slaves. Others went to small schools. Some boys also learnt how to play a musical instrument and were trained in athletics.

In Sparta, boys were taught to fight and most of their school time was spent training to be fit and strong. Spartan girls were also sent to school for physical training.

Source C　　**Source D**　　**Source E**

13 Clothes

Fashion in Ancient Greece did not change as quickly as it does today. Clothes were made by hand and the designs were very simple. They did not need complicated cutting or much stitching.

The most common garments were the *peplos*, the *chiton* and the *himation*.

Chiton

Peplos

Himation

Most clothes were made from wool which was spun and woven at home. Linen was also popular but it had to be brought from places such as Egypt. This made it more expensive than wool. Cotton was not grown by the Ancient Greeks so cotton clothes were rare and also very expensive.

Most vase paintings show people barefoot. The scent bottle below (**Source A**) is shaped like a foot in a sandal. It gives us a clue as to what some Ancient Greeks wore on their feet.

Source A

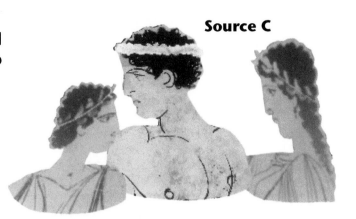

Footwear

Footwear was rarely shown in Ancient Greek art.

1. Can you find any examples of footwear on vase paintings or statues in this book?
2. Is there anything like the sandal above (**Source A**)?

Hairstyles

Most Greek women had long hair.

1. Using **Sources B**, **C** and **D** in this chapter, sketch some of the Ancient Greek hairstyles.
2. What do you notice about how the men wore their hair?

Source D

Sources B

Identifying types of dress

Look again at **Sources B**, **C** and **D**.

1. Which types of dress are these people wearing?
2. Which garments do you think were worn mostly by women?
3. Which were worn mostly by men?

Making a Chiton

To make a chiton you will need:

A felt-tip pen
A large piece of plain material, for example, an old sheet
A needle and thread
A pair of good scissors
A tape measure
Some dressmaker's pins

If you have a sewing machine you will be able to make your chiton fairly quickly, but remember that the Ancient Greeks made all their clothes by hand.

Instructions

1. Cut out a rectangle of material. If you don't have enough material make it a bit shorter or narrower.

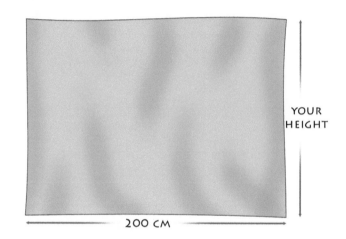

YOUR HEIGHT

200 CM

2. Fold back the edge you have cut. Sew it to stop it fraying. (This will make your chiton last longer, but it may take a long time if you are sewing by hand.)

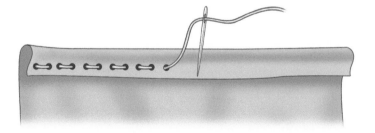

3. Fold the material in half. Pin and sew down one side.

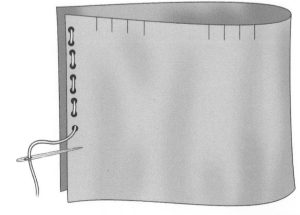

4. Measure along the top edge and make some felt-tip pen marks as shown.

5. Lay your chiton flat on the floor, so that you can see the felt-tip pen marks clearly. Pin the material through the front and back at each of the marks. Try on your chiton carefully to make sure the arm and head holes are big enough. You can ask someone to help you adjust the marks if necessary. Sew six stitches on each of the marks, through the front and back. (You could use safety pins or brooches instead.)

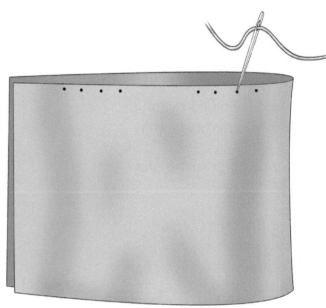

6. Put on your chiton. Cut a strip of material 5 x 150cm (or use an old tie or piece of cord) for a belt. Pull the material above the belt so that your chiton doesn't touch the floor.

7. When you have finished your chiton, do one of the following activities with a friend, or in a small group:
   ● act out a scene from a play
   ● make up and act out a play about a Greek legend
   ● recite some poetry
   ● act out a scene from everyday Greek life.

Greece is a very mountainous country and only about one fifth of the land can be used for farming. However, in Ancient Greece most of the people earned their living by farming. The soil was poor and hard. Wet winters followed by long, hot, dry summers meant that few crops grew. It was difficult to grow enough grass for the animals to eat.

By reading Ancient Greek poems, plays and essays we can find out about what people grew and the animals they kept. Pictures on domestic objects, such as vases and cups, also provide us with evidence.

Source A
A farmer in modern Greece.

A farmer's life

Look at the information in this chapter.

1. Do you think that a farmer's life was "the sweetest life on earth"?
2. What evidence have you used to make your decision?
3. Describe what a farmer's life might have been like.

A Greek poet, Moschus, described a fisherman's life:

A wretched life a fisherman's must be,
His home a ship, his labour in the sea,
And fish, the slippery object of his gain.

Gathering olives from a tree.

Some Greek writers described the farming life:

... here is the season for shearing your sheep of their spring wool.

I feed a thousand sheep, and from them drink excellent milk; and never want for cheese.

The earth smelled of rich summer and autumn fruit: we were ankle-deep in pears, and apples rolled all about our toes. With dark damson plums the young sapling branches trailed on the ground.

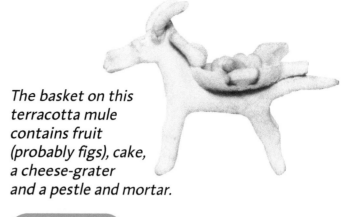

The basket on this terracotta mule contains fruit (probably figs), cake, a cheese-grater and a pestle and mortar.

A woman baking bread.

A bronze statue of a farmer ploughing.

The diet

Read the modern historian's description of the Ancient Greek diet.

1. What evidence confirms this was the usual diet?
2. Can you suggest anything else that might have been eaten?

Farming today

Look at the pictures of modern farming in Greece (**Sources A** and **B**). In some ways farming has not changed very much from ancient times.

1. How do you think a modern farmer's life is different from a farmer's life 2500 years ago?
2. What are the reasons for these differences?

A modern historian describes the diet of the Ancient Greeks:

... stone-ground bread, goat's cheese, a handful of olives and figs, diluted wine, a little honey, some eggs and dried fish, with meat a rarity to be eaten only on feast days ... or some other special occasion.

Source B *Modern farming methods in Greece.*

If you go on holiday to Greece, you will find that most tavernas (Greek restaurants) have greek salad on the menu. Greek salad is not always exactly the same in every taverna, but one common recipe is given below.

Mixed Greek Salad

¼lb feta cheese	1 small onion
½ cucumber	3 tomatoes
½ cup of olive oil	1 tablespoon vinegar
2oz black olives	½ teaspoon salt

1. Cut the tomatoes into quarters.
2. Cut the cucumber into small chunks.
3. Slice the onion thinly.
4. Cut the feta cheese into cubes.
5. Put all the ingredients into a large salad bowl. Mix carefully and serve.

A Greek salad

This salad will be enough for four people to have one small bowl each. Most supermarkets sell the ingredients. See if you can buy the ingredients and make the salad with a group of friends or in the classroom.

Note: An adult should be with you when you are cutting up the food.

Now try the salad!

1. Which ingredients have you not tasted before?
2. Do you like the mixture of tastes?
3. What do you think the salad should be eaten with?

Which ingredients?

Most of the ingredients of this salad would have been used by the Ancient Greeks.

1. Use the quotations opposite and definitions below on this page to find out which ingredients the Ancient Greeks used, and which ingredients they did not have.
2. Now rewrite the recipe to show what kind of salad people might have eaten about 2500 years ago in Greece.

Definitions

Brine: water saturated with common salt.

Tomato: a glossy, fleshy fruit, native of South America. (Europeans first encountered South America in the 15th century CE.)

Feta cheese: a firm white cheese made from sheep's or goat's milk.

Food for thought

Use chapter 14 to work out what an Ancient Greek family might have eaten for one meal.

Complete the lunch menu below.

Quotations

'Do you expect the city to pay you with a tribute of onions?'

(Aristophanes)

'Instead of which you have to queue up for your pay like a lot of olive pickers.'

(Aristophanes)

'Blow on me with thy divine breath
And serve vinegar and brine.'

(Aristophanes)

'I feed a thousand sheep ...
and never want for cheese.'

(Moschus)

'Also cucumbers that are ripe, and pears and apples.'

(Praxilla)

Lunch Menu

Main course:

Dessert:

The Trojan War: Fact or Fiction?

The story of the Trojan War is one of the most famous tales of Ancient Greece. Parts of the story are told in Homer's *Iliad*, as well as in many of the great tragic plays.

For many generations, people thought that the Trojan War was just a story. However, in 1870 an archaeologist called Heinrich Schliemann discovered the ruins of an ancient city. This city was in the same place as the one mentioned by Homer. Schliemann came to believe that there really had been a war between Greece and Troy, and now most modern historians agree with him.

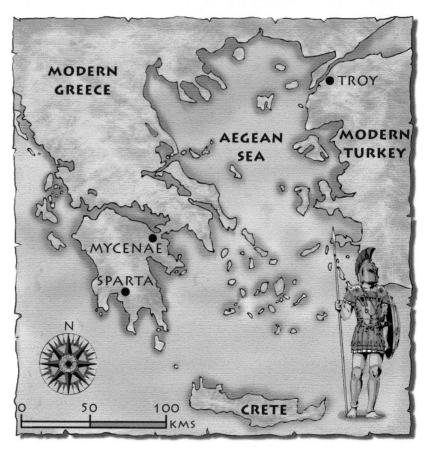

The story of the Trojan War was passed on by word of mouth for hundreds of years before Homer wrote it down in about 800 BCE. When stories are told, rather than written down, they are often a little bit different at each telling. People often like to exaggerate when they tell a story.

True or False?

Read the story of the Trojan War on page 39. You are going to try to decide which parts of the story could be facts (true) and which parts are probably fiction (not true).

Work in small groups.

1. With a coloured pen or highlighter, underline any parts of the story which you think might be true.
2. With a different colour, underline the parts of the story which you think are made-up.

Note: You don't have to underline the whole story. There will be some parts you can't decide about. Work carefully and discuss what you are doing. You should be able to give reasons for your decisions.

The Trojan War

The war between Troy and Greece started because of a Greek woman called Helen. Helen was the daughter of Zeus and Leda, and she was the most beautiful woman in the world. All the Greek princes wanted to marry Helen, but her foster-father chose Menelaus of Sparta to be her husband.

When Prince Paris of Troy came to Sparta, he and Helen fell in love and Helen went back to Troy with him. Menelaus was furious when Helen disappeared. He asked his brother, Agamemnon, and all the princes who had wanted to marry Helen, to help him to get her back. A thousand ships set sail for Troy. When the Greek ships reached Troy, the Trojans refused to return Helen, so the war began.

The war lasted for ten years. The Greeks could not break into Troy and the Trojans could not drive the Greeks away. There were many heroes on each side. One of the great Trojan heroes was Aeneas, son of the goddess Aphrodite. He was wounded by Diomedes, but the deities (gods) carried him away and healed his wounds.

The most famous Greek hero was Achilles, the son of the goddess Thetis. The only place where Achilles could be hurt was on one heel. It was Paris who eventually killed him by shooting him in the heel.

After ten years the Greeks finally broke into Troy by playing a trick on the Trojans. They built a huge wooden horse as a gift to the goddess Athena, so that she would give them a safe journey home.

The Greeks left the wooden horse outside the gates of Troy and then sailed away. The Trojans were very pleased, and they pulled the horse through the city gates to offer it to Athena at their own temple. That night, when the Trojans were asleep, some Greeks who had been hiding inside the horse climbed out. They opened the city gates and let in the Greek army who had sneaked back in the dark. The Greek army destroyed Troy and killed many Trojans. Helen was captured and taken back to Menelaus. The war was over.

(Adapted from Greek Myths and Legends, *Usborne)*

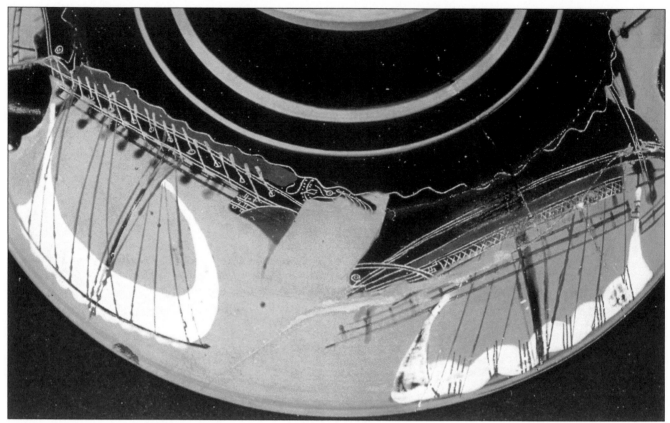

Source A
Ancient Greek trading ship.

The Ancient Greeks could not grow all the crops or produce all the materials that they needed. The landscape and climate were good for growing grapevines and olive trees, but the land was too mountainous to grow enough wheat for the people.

Bread was one of the basic foods for most Greeks, so large amounts of grain had to be imported. Merchants sailed all over the world to buy grain and other goods which the Greeks were unable to produce themselves.

Trading ships

Source A shows a vase painting of an Ancient Greek trading ship.

1. Look at **Source A** and then draw your own picture.
2. Record how the ship was powered, steered and where the cargo might have been kept.
3. Why do you think an eye was painted on the bow of the ship?

Imports

Look carefully at the map in **Source B**. It shows which countries traded with Ancient Greece.

1. List the places which supplied Greece with grain.
2. What other goods were imported and where did they come from?

Travel

Look back at the map of Greece and the pictures of the Greek landscape in chapter 6.

1. Why do you think travelling over land may have been difficult in Ancient Greece?
2. Why did sea travel become very important?

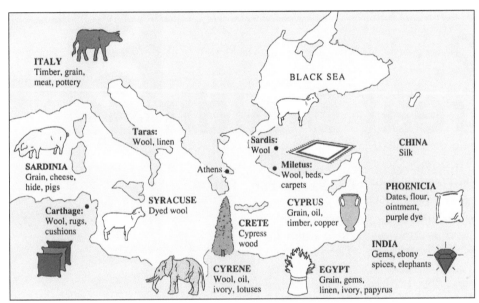

ITALY
Timber, grain, meat, pottery

BLACK SEA

Taras:
Wool, linen

Sardis:
Wool

CHINA
Silk

Athens

Miletus:
Wool, beds, carpets

SARDINIA
Grain, cheese, hide, pigs

PHOENICIA
Dates, flour, ointment, purple dye

Carthage:
Wool, rugs, cushions

SYRACUSE
Dyed wool

CYPRUS
Grain, oil, timber, copper

CRETE
Cypress wood

INDIA
Gems, ebony spices, elephants

CYRENE
Wool, oil, ivory, lotuses

EGYPT
Grain, gems, linen, ivory, papyrus

Source B

Money

Look at the photographs of Ancient Greek coins (**Source C**).

1. Compare them with modern coins. How are they similar?
2. How are they different?
3. How do you think they might have been made?
4. Compare this method with modern coin-making.

The first place to use money was a wealthy state near Greece, called Lydia. The Lydians used flat discs of solid silver and gold to trade for basic goods such as food and wine.

Source C

The Ancient Greeks exported pots, statues, oil and wine. In early times, there was no money and the Greeks swapped these goods for other things that they needed.

18 Great Buildings

Although little remains of Ancient Greek houses (see chapter 8), the ruins of some public buildings still stand today. These buildings were made from hard, strong materials, such as marble and limestone. The stones were fixed together with metal bolts and pegs. The buildings were strong enough to withstand thousands of years of weathering.

Identifying the buildings

Look carefully at **Sources A** and **B**.

1. Which do you think is:
   – the Theatre of Dionysus?
   – the Temple of Aphaia?
2. Think of words to describe these buildings.

Source A

Source B

Source C

Source D

Source E

Let us take a closer look at the remains of one public building. The picture below shows the Parthenon in Athens. It was a temple built in honour of the goddess Athena.

The Ancient Greeks were very proud of their public buildings and they spent a great deal of time, money and energy building them. The Parthenon took 15 years to build.

pediment
carvings
lintel
capital
column

Source F
The Elgin Marbles.

The design of the Parthenon was simple. A line of elegant columns ran round the outside of the building, supporting lintels. These lintels were decorated with stone carvings. At each end of the building the lintels were topped with stone triangles called pediments.

There were many different architectural styles in Ancient Greece. The Parthenon was designed in the Doric style. This meant that the capitals were plain and the columns sturdy and undecorated at the base.

In the Inner Temple, a continuous, carved frieze ran round the top of the building. These carvings were of fantastic creatures, deities and heroes from Greek myths and legends. They are now known as the Elgin Marbles.

The Elgin Marbles were named after the Earl of Elgin who lived in the 18th century. His name was Thomas Bruce, and when he visited Greece he was greatly impressed by the beauty of the Parthenon. The ruins were crumbling so Elgin decided to make drawings and plaster casts of the carvings. Then he started to collect pieces of the frieze and had them shipped back to Britain.

These statues and carvings are now in the British Museum in London, but there has been a lot of discussion about whether they should stay in Britain or be sent back to Greece.

The Elgin Marbles

The Elgin Marbles shown in **Source F** are of great historical and artistic value.

1. Do you think that Thomas Bruce was right to bring pieces of the Parthenon to Britain in the 18th Century?
2. Do you think the carvings really belong to the British or the Greeks?
3. What do you think should happen to the collection now?
4. Look at **Sources C**, **D** and **E**. What can you see in these carvings?

The Ancient Greeks believed in many deities. They believed that the 12 most important deities were all part of one family who lived on the top of a great mountain called Mount Olympus. These 12 deities were called the Olympians.

There is a large amount of evidence about the Olympian deities. Temples were built in their honour. Statues of them were made for people to worship, and Greek stories and plays are full of tales about them.

Zeus, the king of the Olympian deities.

A model of the Temple of Zeus at Olympia.

The statue below (**Source A**) is of Aphrodite (called Venus by the Romans), the goddess of love and beauty. The statue is called the Venus de Milo and can be found in the Louvre Museum in Paris. It is probably the most famous statue from Ancient Greece in the world today.

The Greek gods and goddesses were believed to be immortal (have everlasting life), but in other ways they were like humans. For example, they could fall in love, argue, be happy, angry, sad and jealous.

The Greeks told many stories about their deities and used them to explain things in the natural world which they did not understand.

One of the most famous myths is about Pluto, the god of the Underworld. He fell in love and kidnapped Persephone, daughter of Demeter. Demeter was goddess of all plants, and when Persephone was kidnapped she neglected her plants to search for her daughter. This caused winter. Eventually, Persephone was allowed to return to her mother for six months of every year, bringing spring and summer with her.

The role of the deities

Each of the Olympian deities had a special responsibility in the world.

1. Read the four extracts below. They are all taken from Greek plays. Decide who was:
   - the god of the sea
   - the god of music
   - the goddess of hunting and the moon
   - the god of the weather.

"Artemis,
Daughter of Zeus and huntress,
Queen of shades,
Guiding the light in darkness … "

"Listen, Apollo, you who can wake to song
The seven strings of your lifeless lyre,
Till they chant immortal music to lonely shepherds …"

"Zeus, you sovereign of thunder,
Shiver him with lightning."

"Come, dread Poseidon, ruler of the salty oceans;
Forsake thy deep hiding-places
In the fish-filled, frenzied sea."

Source A
Venus de Milo

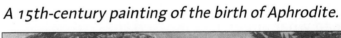

A 15th-century painting of the birth of Aphrodite.

Source A
The myth of Helios.

The Ancient Greeks loved to tell and listen to stories. Some of the stories were connected to religious beliefs and these stories are called myths. They explained things in the natural world, such as the seasons, earthquakes and thunder. Myths also explained what angered or pleased the deities.

Some Ancient Greek stories were based on real events and people. These are called legends.

One famous legend is about Oedipus, a prince of Thebes. Oedipus was adopted at birth, and when he grew up he unknowingly killed his father and married his mother. When he discovered what he had done he blinded himself and fled from Thebes.

Most of the stories were told rather than read. We still know some of the stories today because after many years they were written down. Sometimes they were written as poems, and sometimes as plays.

Helios

Look at the vase painting shown in **Source A**. It illustrates the myth of Helios, who drove his chariot of the sun across the sky from east to west every day.

1. What did this myth try to explain?
2. We use the word 'heliosis' today. Look it up in a dictionary and explain where the word comes from.

Homer wrote two epics (very long poems) called the *Odyssey* and the *Iliad*. The *Odyssey* tells the story of Odysseus and his adventures as he returns home after fighting in the Trojan War. The painting below (**Source B**) shows one of his adventures.

Source B

One of Odysseus' many adventures.

Orestes killing Aegisthus.

Find out about myths and legends

Below is a list of some famous Greek myths and legends.

1. Find out about these stories:
   – Theseus and the Minotaur
   – Helen of Troy
   – Jason and the Argonauts
   – King Midas
   – Narcissus.
2. Which of these stories do you think are myths and which are legends?
3. Choose a dramatic scene from one of these stories and draw a picture of it.

Theseus and his deeds.

Aeschylus wrote three plays which tell the tragic legend of King Agamemnon and his family. King Agamemnon was killed in his bath by his wife Clytemnestra. Years later, their son Orestes, killed Clytemnestra and her new husband, Aegisthus. The plays tell of these murders and of what happened to the family afterwards.

According to Greek legend, Theseus was the son of Aegus, king of Athens. He performed many brave deeds. He killed the Minotaur, a fierce monster who lived in a maze called the labyrinth in Crete.

How do people spend their leisure today?

Think what people do with their leisure today.

1. Interview some adults to get as many ideas as possible.
2. Decide whether most of the activities are done alone, with one other person, or with a group.
3. Draw up a chart like the one below and fill it in.

Activity	Alone	With one person	With a group
Tennis			
Dancing			

4. **Source B** shows Achilles and Ajax playing a game. What game do you think it may have been?

Source B

Achilles and Ajax playing a game.

People in Ancient Greece also enjoyed their leisure. In this chapter you can see some of the ways in which they spent their free time.

Dinner parties were very popular among men. It was a time for them to meet, talk and enjoy good food. They were served by their slaves. Wives were not invited to these parties, but the men paid women dancers to come and entertain them. Often at their parties, the men made up poems and riddles, listened to musicians, or watched acrobats.

Source A   *Musicians, dancers and acrobats were hired to entertain men at dinner parties.*

Music was very important to some of the Ancient Greeks. The sons and daughters of rich citizens were usually taught how to play an instrument. We do not know how Greek music sounded because very little written music has been found.

Source D
A theatrical scene.

The Greeks loved to tell and listen to stories. Poetry was also very popular. Poems were recited at festivals and parties by men called rhapsodies.

The Greeks also enjoyed going to the theatre to see plays. You can find out more about Ancient Greek plays in the next chapter.

Source C
Rich Ancient Greek citizens were often taught how to play an instrument.

Entertainment for the rich and poor

Some of the leisure activities in this chapter were only enjoyed by wealthy people.

Which activities could have been enjoyed by everyone?

How did the Ancient Greeks spend their leisure?

Look at all the sources in this chapter and the next.

1. Draw up a chart to show all the different activities and decide whether they were done alone, with one other person, or in a group.
2. Compare your chart with the one drawn up about modern activities. Are there any similarities? Why are some activities different?
3. Which Ancient Greek activity would you have enjoyed?

Going to the theatre was a very important part of Ancient Greek life. Many theatres were built and hundreds of plays were performed.

There were many famous dramatists (people who wrote plays), such as Euripides, Aeschylus, Sophocles (who wrote tragedies), and Aristophanes (who wrote comedies). Tragedies were serious plays which told well-known stories of kings and queens, heroes and heroines. The comedies were usually very up-to-date. They often made fun of famous politicians or other dramatists.

In Athens, plays were written for a festival in honour of the god Dionysus. People went to the festival to watch four or five plays at a time. Judges had to decide which play was the best.

Source A

Sophocles

Comedies

The vase painting in **Source A** shows a scene from a comic play. Can you work out what is happening?

Lost plays

Many plays were written in Ancient Greece, but most have been lost.

Why do you think this is? (Clue: think about what the plays might have been written on and the number of copies probably made of each play.)

50

Look at the photograph of the theatre of Dionysus in **Source B**.

Discuss and decide:
– where the audience sat
– where the actors acted the play
– why the theatre was shaped as it was
– where the judges sat.

Source B *The theatre of Dionysus in Athens.*

Source C
Theatre masks reconstructed to look like the original ones used in Ancient Greece.

Plays written in Ancient Greece are still performed today. They have been translated into many languages so they can be performed all over the world. People still laugh at the jokes in the comedies and are still fascinated by the terrible stories told in the tragedies.

There were only a few actors who played the main parts in a Greek play. They often had to play more than one part. There was also a chorus of actors who spoke and moved together.

The actors were always men, so they had to play female roles as well as male roles. Large masks were worn to show which character they were playing.

Masks

Look at the pictures of the masks in **Source C**. They were usually caricatures (exaggerated pictures) of the characters.

Why do you think the masks were so exaggerated and so large?

Models of comic actors.

In Ancient Greece, athletics was one of the most popular sports for men because it kept them fit. This meant that they would be in a good condition to fight if war broke out.

The Olympic Games was one of four major sporting events which attracted competitors from all over the Greek world. These games were held every four years at Olympia in honour of the god Zeus. They lasted for five days. Messengers travelled to all the major Greek cities to announce the Games and all the wars had to end to allow the athletes to travel to Olympia in safety.

Buildings for the Olympic Games

Special buildings were built at Olympia for the Games. Look carefully at **Source A** below which shows how they might have looked.

Decide which buildings were:
- the Temple of Zeus
- the stadium for running races
- the gymnasium.

Source A *A model of the Ancient Olympic buildings.*

The events

We can see evidence on vases of the kind of events which took place.

1. Look at **Sources B**, **C**, **D** and **E** and identify the different events.
2. Do we have the same events in the modern Olympic Games?
3. The hand-held weight in **Source E** was used by long-jumpers. Can you guess why?

Source B

Women were not allowed to take part in the Olympic Games. They held their own games at Olympia in honour of Hera, Zeus' wife. There was only one event. What do you think it was, judging by the statue below?

Source C

Source D

Source E

It was considered an honour simply to compete in the Games. Individual winners were presented with olive wreaths, palm branches or ribbons.

The last Ancient Olympic Games was held about 1600 years ago. Earthquakes and floods then destroyed the site of Olympia. It was not until the last century that archaeologists discovered the site. In 1896, the first modern Olympic Games was held in Athens.

The time before people began to write is called prehistory. The only way we can find out about prehistoric times is by looking at the remains of buildings and artefacts. This makes it difficult for historians to get detailed information about life during these times.

The Ancient Greeks began to read and write very early on in their civilisation. This means that we can use what they wrote as evidence of their lives and way of thinking.

Some of the work of the great writers has survived, but most of it has been lost. The Ancient Greeks did not write, print and publish books to sell to lots of people as we do today. Instead, they wrote everything by hand. There were usually just a few copies of each piece of work. They were probably written on papyrus, which is a type of paper made from reeds.

The great writers

Here are the names of some of the great writers:

Homer   Aristophanes
Herodotus   Plato.

1. Look at chapters 20, 22 and 26 to find out what each of them wrote.
2. What do you think might have happened to the work that didn't survive?

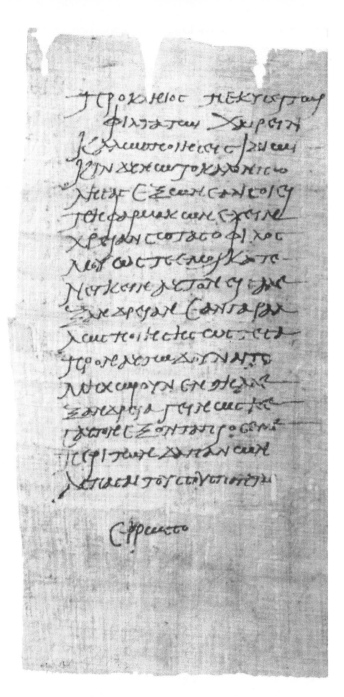

Here is a letter written in Greek on papyrus.

Ivory pen.

As well as writing great plays and poems, the Ancient Greeks used writing in their everyday lives. Ivory pens such as the one shown on page 54 were used to scratch words on wax tablets.

Some people wrote down the great tales which had been passed down from generation to generation through story telling. Others wrote down what they had learnt about history, mathematics and science.

Examining the evidence

Wax tablets were useful for writing on because they could be used over and over again. The flat end of pens could smooth over the wax once the writing was no longer needed.

1. What sort of people do you think wrote with pens and wax tablets? (Clue: read the extract by Herodas below.)
2. What might they have been writing?
3. Who else may have found wax tablets useful?

In a poem by Herodas, a mother complained about her son to his schoolmaster.

His slighted writing tablet,
Which every month I take to wax,
Is left to be forgotten against the wall
Under his bed ... unless he scowls in rage
As though it were his death and
Scrapes it bare instead of writing upon it.

Comparing alphabets

Look carefully at the examples of Greek writing in this chapter.

1. Make a copy of all the letters that are like English letters.
2. Can you find any letters that are completely different to those in the English alphabet?

The Ancient Greeks also used marble and bronze to write on. They were generally used to record public messages, laws, lists of winners in competitions and so on. These plaques could be hung up in public places such as the agora.

This inscription is part of an agreement between Athens and another city state.

When we read things that the Ancient Greeks wrote, we are usually reading a translation. The Greek alphabet is not the same as our alphabet, although many of our letters come from it. The word 'alphabet' comes from the Greek words 'alpha' and 'beta'.

Ancient Greek words

Many English words derive (come from) Ancient Greek ones, for example:
- geography
- history
- telephone
- microscope
- hypodermic.

Can you find any more?

Here are some Greek words and their meanings:

tele = far off	*peri* = around	*micro* = small
phone = voice	*mega* = great	*stetho* = chest
photo = light	*graph* = written	*scope* = look at

Explaining words

Many English words come from the Ancient Greek language. Some of these words are made-up of two Greek words put together.

1. Look at the list of scientific inventions in the chart below.
2. Look up the name of each invention in the dictionary and write the definition in the first column.
3. In the second column, write the real meaning of the word from the Greek.
4. Write down any other words you can think of that start or end with one of the Greek words above.

Invention	What the dictionary says	The Greek meaning
megaphone	large speaking trumpet for carrying sound of voice to a distance	great voice
telephone		
telescope		
telegraph		
microphone		
microscope		
stethoscope		
periscope		
photograph		

Below are some words about school and school activities. They all come from Greek words and the Greek meanings are given.

Word	Greek meaning
Mathematics	something learned
History	to learn or know by inquiry
Geography	writing about the Earth
School	leisure
Cylinder	roller
Sphere	ball
Meter	measure

How well do you think the English meanings of the words fit the original Greek meanings?

GREEK

Α	Β	Γ	Δ	Ε	Ζ	Η	Θ	Ι	Κ	Λ	Μ	Ν	Ξ	Ο	Π	Ρ	Σ	Τ	Υ	Φ	Χ	Ψ	Ω
A	B	G	D	E	Z	E,H	TH	I	C,K	L	M	N	X	O	P	R,RH	S	T	Y,U	PH	CH	PS	O

ENGLISH

Comparing alphabets

The table above shows two alphabets. The top line is the alphabet that was used in Classical Greece, and the bottom line is the English alphabet we use today. You can see that some of the letters are the same, but many are different.

1. Using the table, write the names of the following famous people in Greek:
   ● Euripides
   ● Aristotle
   ● Sappho
   ● Herodotus

2. Now write the names of these deities and heroes in Greek:
   ● Achilles
   ● Heracles
   ● Athena
   ● Dionysus

3. If you look at vase paintings, you may be able to find these, or other names, painted beside people in the pictures. See if you can work out who the people are.

Source A *Herodotus*

Source B *Archimedes*

In the early years of Greek civilisation, people believed that the deities were responsible for everything that happened in the world. They were thought to control natural things, such as the weather and earthquakes, as well as the lives of people. The past was explained by myths which were part of the religious beliefs of the time.

However, as time went on, many people began to look for more logical and practical explanations for things which happened in the world around them. People also began to record their thoughts and discoveries. These people are known as philosophers, which means 'lovers of knowledge'.

The Ancient Greek philosophers studied many different subjects and developed ideas and ways of working that we still use today. Some of the greatest thinkers in Ancient Greece are featured in this chapter.

Herodotus was an historian. He found out about the past by travelling to places where important events had taken place. He asked people what they had seen and heard. Herodotus is known as 'the father of history'. In Greek, 'historie' means 'to learn or know by questioning'.

Archimedes invented a system for irrigating and draining land. The system is known as 'Archimedes' Screw'.

Source C *Hippocrates*

Hippocrates was a doctor. He was one of the first doctors to believe that illness has natural causes. Hippocrates also wrote about how doctors should behave towards their patients.

Here are some of Hippocrates' observations and advice:

Should one part of the body be hotter or colder than the rest, disease is present in that part.

Cold is bad for the bones, teeth, nerves, brain and the spinal cord: heat is good for these structures.

Milk is not recommended for those who suffer from headaches.

Those who are bald do not suffer from varicose veins.

Anaximander was interested in how the universe began. He believed that humans had developed from another kind of animal, possibly a fish or dolphin.

Source D *Euclid*

Euclid was a mathematician. He introduced ideas such as an angle in geometry.

A doctor's opinion

Read the statements made by Hippocrates.

1. Which points do you think modern doctors would agree with?
2. Which points do you think modern doctors would disagree with?

Our ancestors

Anaximander believed that humans had evolved (developed) over a long period of time.

This theory was re-stated by Charles Darwin in Victorian Britain. Find out what the public's reaction was in the 19th century.

Aristotle is one of the most famous philosophers and among his many projects, he invented a system for classifying animals and plants.

Plato was a pupil of Socrates. He had many ideas about how an ideal state should be run.

Source E *Aristotle*

Source F *Plato*

Anaxagoras believed that the Sun was a flaming mass and that the moon's light was reflected from the Sun.

It is said that Aristarchus believed that the Earth turned on its axis and that it moved around the Sun. We cannot be sure that this is true, because Aristarchus never wrote his ideas down.

Pythagoras worked out ideas in mathematics. His theory about triangles is quite complicated, but it is still used today.

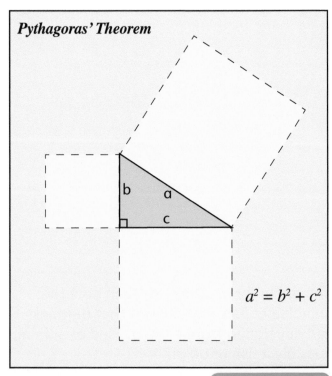

Pythagoras' Theorem

$$a^2 = b^2 + c^2$$

Judging the evidence

Look at **Sources A–G** in this chapter.

1. Which do you think were done in Ancient Greek times?
2. How can you tell?

The Philosophers

Thucydides was an Athenian historian who wrote about the Peloponnesian War. He served as a general during the war.

Source G *Thucydides*

Ideas new and old

Look through the ideas expressed by the philosophers in this chapter.

1. Which ideas do we still believe in today?
2. Have any ideas developed or changed?
3. Choose two of the philosophers on these pages and find out more about what they wrote and said.

Socrates was a philosopher who often questioned other people's beliefs. He was unpopular with the politicians of Athens and was eventually sentenced to death.

Socrates in prison, surrounded by his followers.

During the first century BCE, the Roman army invaded Greece and made it part of the Roman Empire. The Romans were impressed by many Greek ideas and they copied them. They stole statues, pots and other works of art from houses and temples and took them back to Italy. They also captured Greek people to be slaves and to help teach their children. This helped to spread Greek ideas to other parts of the world.

Although the Ancient Greeks lived 2500 years ago, and on the other side of Europe, their civilisation still influences us today. It is not only western Europe, but nations all over the world who have benefited from the legacy of Ancient Greece.

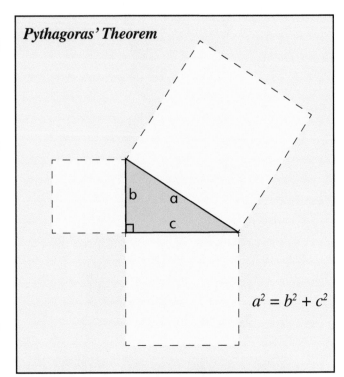

Pythagoras' Theorem

$$a^2 = b^2 + c^2$$

Source A

Source B

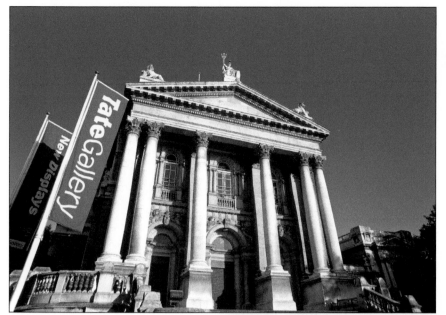

Source C

Where do these words come from?

Look up these words in a dictionary to find out where they come from:
- hypodermic
- polygon
- telescope
- microcosm.

Source D

Source E

Connecting past and present

Look at all the sources in this chapter. Each shows a connection between our world and the Ancient Greek world.

Discuss the connection in each source. You may find it helpful to look back through the book to remind yourself of some of the things you have learnt.

Index